Whose Is This?

Written by Narinder Dhami
Illustrated by Victor Tavares

ISBN-13: 978-0-328-83278-1
ISBN-10: 0-328-83278-2
7   18

Contents

Chapter One   4

Chapter Two   10

Chapter Three   19

Chapter Four   24

Chapter One

It was the second day of the town culture fair. People had come together to celebrate and share the different foods and traditions of their cultures.

Maria and her friend Kimi were going to the fair with Maria's mom and dad. They were really excited to visit all the booths and find out more about their neighbors!

When Maria, her parents, and Kimi arrived at the fair, they saw people selling delicious food at some of the stands.

"I want to try *all* the different foods!" laughed Kimi.

There was also music, dancing, and storytelling. Everywhere Maria and Kimi looked, they saw color and movement. Some people were wearing beautiful clothes from other countries.

"This is so much fun," Maria said. "I can't wait to start walking around!"

"We'll walk around the fair later," said Maria's dad. "First, your mom and I are working at the information stand. We'll be helping people find their way around the fair. You girls can come and help us."

Maria and Kimi looked disappointed. They wanted to explore right away. But they agreed to help out at the information stand.

Maria and Kimi gave maps of the fair to people passing by. But soon they got a little bored.

"You can fold these for me," said Maria's mom, handing them a stack of maps. Maria and Kimi sat underneath the table folding maps. They watched people's feet going past.

"Everyone's having more fun than we are!" Kimi said sadly.

"I know," said Maria. She folded a map into a paper plane and threw it at Kimi. Kimi gasped and then she laughed. Soon they were both in fits of giggles.

"What are you two doing under there?" said Maria's mom as she peered under the table. "Stop causing mischief!"

The girls reluctantly crawled out from under the table and went to stand behind it. Then something on the ground caught Kimi's eye.

Chapter Two

It was a box, and it was full of interesting and colorful objects. But Maria and Kimi didn't know what any of them were.

"Look what we found, Mom," said Maria.

"That's the lost and found box," said Maria's mom. "Most of those things were lost yesterday. Mrs. Rodriguez, the woman handing out maps yesterday, told me she couldn't find out who owned them. She didn't even know what some of them were. Actually . . . neither do I!"

"I have a great idea, Maria," Kimi said. "Why don't we try to find the people who lost these things?"

"Can we, Mom?" asked Maria.

"I guess you girls can do a little exploring," said Maria's mom. "Just don't go too far."

"Yes! Let's do it!" Maria laughed. She held out the box to Kimi. "You choose the first thing!"

Kimi closed her eyes and pulled something out of the box. It was a long, orange cloth.

The cloth went on, and on, and on. The girls thought it would never end!

"What is it?" asked Maria.

"Maybe it's a tablecloth," Kimi replied.

"But it's not the right shape," Maria said. "Let's walk around and see if we can find out what it is."

The girls walked around the stands
looking for clues. They passed by their
neighbors' stands. Mr. Obi, their Nigerian
neighbor, was selling his goat curry. His
wife was next to him, wearing a bright
blue headwrap. But it wasn't like the
orange cloth.

Then they came to an Indian stand.
A woman wearing a beautiful sari was
selling bangles and bindis.

"Maria," Kimi said excitedly. "I think
this cloth might be a sari!"

The woman overheard Kimi and smiled.

"It's not quite the right shape for a sari,"
she said. "But I think it *might* belong to my
husband! Does that give you a clue?"

The girls were puzzled. Then they heard
a voice over the loudspeaker.

"The turban-tying competition is
starting *right now!* Show us how quickly
you can tie your turban!"

Some men went past, carrying rolls of brightly colored cloth.

"I know!" Maria cried, holding up the orange cloth. "It's a turban!"

"You're right!" the woman laughed. "Lots of Indian men wear turbans. My husband wanted to enter the competition, but he lost his turban. Thank you for returning it!"

Maria and Kimi watched the turban-tying competition. The men wrapped the turbans around their heads very quickly. The winner did it in just six minutes!

"Awesome!" Maria said.

"I wonder what else is in the lost and found box," said Kimi. They headed back to the information stand.

Chapter Three

Now it was Maria's turn to choose. She closed her eyes and pulled something out of the box.

"It's a stick!" said Maria.

"Maybe it's a musical instrument," Kimi said.

Maria tried to blow into the stick, but no sound came out. The girls walked around the fair, asking the people behind the booths about the stick. But no one knew what it was for.

"Maybe it's a toy," said Maria.

Then Kimi spotted Moki, a Lakota boy from their school.

"Hey, Moki," she called. "Look at this stick we found!"

Moki grinned and took the stick. "It's my grandfather's," he said. "He lost it yesterday. Do you know what it is, Kimi?" Moki gave the stick to Kimi.

"Is it a musical instrument?" asked Kimi.

"No!" Moki said, taking the stick. "Do you know, Maria?" He gave her the stick.

"Is it a toy?" said Maria. "Or a walking stick?"

Moki took the stick back. "Wrong!" he said.

"Why do you keep giving us the stick and taking it back?" asked Maria.

"Because only the person holding the stick can talk?" Kimi guessed.

"Yes, it's a *talking stick!*" Moki laughed. "When Native American people like the Lakota have meetings, only the person with the stick can speak."

"That's so cool!" Maria said.

The girls said good-bye to Moki and returned to the information stand.

"Let's see what else is in the box!" Maria said. "It's your turn, Kimi."

Kimi closed her eyes and pulled something from the box.

Chapter Four

Kimi pulled out a small case of shiny, polished wood. The girls opened it. Inside were twelve round hollows carved into the wood.

"I think it's a party dish," said Maria. "You put nuts in it!"

"Maybe it's a jewelry box," said Kimi. The girls set out walking around the stands again. They talked to Kimi's neighbor, Madame Fontaine, who was selling her homemade French pastries. But she didn't know what the case was.

The girls talked to more and
more people, but no one knew
what the wooden case was for.

"Maybe it's to keep marbles in," Maria said.

Suddenly Kimi looked down. She saw a blue stone lying at her feet. She picked it up.

"Look, there's another," said Maria, pointing at the ground. "And another!"

The girls followed the trail. There were twelve blue stones and they led to some tables where lots of children were playing the same board game.

Each of the wooden boards had twelve holes filled with stones or seeds.

"Oh, you found my son's Oware Nam Nam game!" said a woman in Ghanaian dress. "Children in West Africa love Oware Nam Nam."

"Can we play?" Kimi asked.

"Of course," said the woman. She showed the girls how to play the game.

Maria and Kimi had a fun time playing Oware Nam Nam.

When they got back to the information stand, Maria peeped inside the box.

"There's one thing left, Kimi," Maria said. "And I don't know what it is!"

The last thing at the bottom of the box was made of shiny metal. It was round and looked a bit heavy, and it had a lid.

"It looks like a frying pan," said Kimi.

"But the handle's all wrong!" Maria replied with a frown.

The girls walked around the fair. They showed the strange metal object to everyone they met.

No one knew what it was. At last they went back to the information stand.

"We don't know who lost this, Mom," Maria said.

Maria's mom smiled.

"That belongs to your grandma!" she said.

Just then Maria's grandma came up to them.

"I want to start making tortillas to sell at our booth," Grandma said. "But I've lost my tortilla press!"

"Here it is, Grandma!" Maria laughed.

"Oh, thank you," Grandma said. "The press makes my tortillas nice and thin."

"Can we come and watch you make tortillas, Grandma?" Maria asked.

"And maybe eat some of them too?" Kimi added.

Grandma chuckled. "Of course," she said. "Tortillas for my young detectives!"